7 Steps to Deliverance

From Darkness to Light

Michael Brown

outskirtspress

DENVER, COLORADO

Outskirts Press, Inc.
http://www.outskirtspress.com

ISBN: 978-1-4787-2420-9

Outskirts Press and the "OP" logo are trademarks belonging to Outskirts Press, Inc.

PRINTED IN THE UNITED STATES OF AMERICA

Table of Contents

Introduction

This is a faith-based self help book for anyone who is suffering from an addiction of sorts and considering a change in life, offering hope through Jesus Christ; or if you are already a Christian, it will help strengthen your walk with the Lord and allow you to grow into maturity. This book offers hope for the hopeless. I offer my own personal testimony of triumph over drugs, alcohol, sexual promiscuities, etc; it will show that, through Christ, you can overcome any obstacle in life, just as I overcame twenty seven plus years of addiction. I am now teaching and preaching the Word of God to others and have started my own business as well, not to mention writing this book, in the process of building my relationship with the Lord. Not that I've been without my trials by any means. But because God is perfect, full of grace and mercy, faithful in His work of deliverance,

I have been able to transform my life from a self destructive life to one of a productive life through Jesus Christ.

The scripture references in this book were taken from the King James Version and the New Living Translation of the Holy Bible. There have been also references from Dictionary.com.

1

First, let me mention the root of our problem:

"In the beginning God created the Heavens and the Earth" **Genesis 1:1,** "Then came Adam, who, after listening to the voice of his wife Eve, fell out of fellowship with God, disobeying a direct command not to eat of the tree of the knowledge of good and evil, and committed the first act of sin, <u>disobedience</u>, separating us all from being in a right relationship with God: **See Genesis 3. Romans 5:12**; says that "as by one man (Adam) sin entered into the world, and death (spiritual separation from God) by sin; and so death passed upon all men, for that all have sinned"

<u>**Sin is defined as**</u>: A transgression against a divine law, a willful violation of some religious or moral principle.

Some would still want to question the validity of this transgression and it may not seem fair that we all have to suffer for someone else's sin, but the fact will still remain that we all have violated, indirectly, the command of God! To help you to understand this error of man I have to take you back to the beginning of the book of Genesis. Adam, meaning ground, was the first out of all creation who was formed from the dust of the ground. God took six days to create everything in heaven and in earth. The sixth day man was formed, and the God said in **Genesis 1:26** "Let us make man in our image, after our likeness......" This image refers to the quality or attributes of God instead of the actual person of God because God is a Spirit; not a physical being. Man is the only creation of God that He placed the breath of life in, "and man became a living soul." **Genesis 2:7**. We have all been born into this same image of man today and unfair as it may be, we all have fallen into the same dispensation as Adam. **Romans 3:23** says that; "All have sinned, and come short of the glory of God." There are many beliefs that will tell you how to rectify this sin issue, but there's only one sacrifice that substantiates that belief, that's through the shed blood on Calvary's Hill by Jesus Christ. Throughout the Old Testament of the Bible we see many types of blood sacrificial offerings taking place; such as sin offerings, peace offerings, grain offerings etc; these offerings were designed only to point us to the sacrificial death of Jesus Christ who became the ultimate sacrifice for our sins that would atone us back into a right relationship with God. **Hebrews 9:22** sums it all up: "And almost all things are by the law purged with blood; and without shedding of blood is no remission (forgiveness) on sin." The Old Testament never could have did the actual job of making things right with God, but only pointed us to believe that some day there would be a sacrifice worthy of accepting. Of course it would take something on our part to do. It takes us to honestly acknowledge our part in this act of sin. **Psalms 51:5** is King David's confession of his sin and repentance to God after he had committed adultery (sin) with Bathsheba; "Behold, I was shapen in iniquity; and in sin did my mother conceive me." David confessed that in his conception from birth he was a sinner, and this took place thousands of years after the fall in the Garden of Eden and thousands of years before Jesus Christ came to be the ultimate sacrifice for our sins. So you see it's nothing we did directly that has caused us all to be in a state of separation from God; however the good news is: Jesus came as the second Adam to shed His blood on Calvary's Hill and to set the record straight.

He offers a second chance for us to make things right with our lives and our relationship with God. **I Corinthians 15:21, 22** says; "For since by man (Adam) came death, (spiritual separation from God) by man (Jesus) came also the resurrection of the dead (spiritually deprived). **V. 22** for as in Adam all die, even so in Christ shall all be made alive. **(All who receive Christ as their Lord and Savior)**

This whole idea of sin and death became real to me when I got saved at age 36. Yet, I wasn't willing to completely give up the life of sin I was living. Of course I didn't fully understand the concept of all the "blood sacrifice or sin" mentioned in the Bible. In **Hebrews 11:25** it mentions "Suffering affliction with the people of God, than to enjoy the pleasures of sin for a season." Well, I wasn't at the point of suffering affliction with the people of God at that point; but I was enjoying the pleasures of sin, and it was just for a season. By the time I got saved, I had been living those "pleasures of sin" out in my life for some twenty plus years and sin became so much a part of my life as the limbs of my body. It seemed impossible to me, naturally, to break away from something I had been accustomed to living for so long. In fact, I told myself on several occasions, "I'm going to die doing these drugs!" I'm sure someone can relate to this! Not that I wanted to die, I just didn't know of a way out. Something inside of me, even before I got saved, cried out! I just didn't Know at the time who to cry out to!

I went into several different rehab centers for detox, which normally lasted about thirty days, some longer. I would hit AA/CA/NA meetings frequently and did so for years, but there was still this void within, feeling something was missing! I thought the void was just the absence of the drugs in my life during the time I was sober. I had never really worked the 12 Steps required by those groups, but I did read them and thought allot about the process required by those groups. Still, I felt something wasn't adequate even within those steps. I honestly thought I couldn't live without the drugs in my life even after some time of being sober while I was in those institutions.

As I began to pray and study God's Word, I ran across a scripture in **Matthew 12:43-46**. It told me something that was hard to understand at the time, but as time went on, the understanding became clearer as to the reasons I kept returning to drugs; and it gave me incite into the possibility of becoming free from drugs and other vices that were holding me in bondage and stunting my growth in life. I didn't fully understand spiritual things, but those verses in Matthew talked about spirits, specifically unclean spirits, and in my case those spirits were drugs. These unclean spirits went out of a man, seeking someplace else to go and they found none. So the unclean spirit decided to return to the place it left! It returned and found that person to be clean from drugs, or whatever was holding him hostage, yet he replaced nothing that was life changing in the place where the unclean spirit was initially. When the unclean spirit noticed that the person placed nothing within him, the spirit went and found "seven other spirits more wicked than himself and entered the man again and the last state or condition of that man became worse than the first time that the unclean spirit was in the man." That's the progression of an addiction or sin. Over time the condition doesn't get better; it only grows worse. There may be a time of sobriety for, a year, two years or twenty years, it doesn't matter. If you don't replace that spirit with something that will change your life for the better, you're wasting time. During times in my sobriety I found myself placing other people, things, places, or whatever in my life to appease me, but none of those things were life changing. **Romans 6:16** says; "Know ye not, that to whom ye yield yourselves servants to obey, his servants ye are to whom ye obey; whether of sin unto death, or of obedience unto righteousness?" After looking at **Matthew 12:43-46** in the perspective of a spiritual nature, I could better understand what I was up against. It still took several years before I was completely free from that life style, but I never gave up. I held onto the promise of God that "He would never leave me nor forsake me," **Hebrews 13:5,** and He has been true to His Word!

My life was becoming so unmanageable I became desperate. I know after a few years of being saved that something still wasn't right within me. I felt a void, even though I had been saved for some time now. Knowing what the problem was is just the beginning of the healing process. Once you know the problem, it's time to find the answer to the problem. For me that took finding out what God's will was for my life. The only way I was able to do that was through the Word of God, The Holy Bible. Remember as I mentioned earlier that we were made in the image of God! To me that meant I needed to go to the source of who created me for the answers I so desperately needed. I had to come to an understanding beyond what I was able to conceive in the natural.

The Bible says in **2 Timothy 3:16,17**; "All scripture is given by inspiration of God, and is profitable for doctrine, for reproof, for correction, for instruction in righteousness **v.17**, That the man of God may be perfect, thoroughly furnished unto all good works." The NLT or New Living Translation puts it this way: "All Scripture is inspired (God breathed) by God and is useful to teach us what is true and to make us realize what is wrong in our lives. It corrects us when we are wrong and teaches us to do what is right. **V.17**, God uses it to prepare and equip his people to do every good work. Of course good works weren't on my agenda at that time, but I wanted to know how I would go about reaching that point in doing good works.

Let me share some insight on my personal experience with 12 step AA/NA/CA groups. Although the counsel is maintaining sobriety through abstinence, there is yet still a void in the life of most people recovering from an addiction. There are some unresolved issues that still remain. I believe it's fair to say that for the most part the drugs were not the primary problems in a person's life. More often than not, it was something else that was encountered in life that lead us to the addiction. Once we're sober, there is yet the initial problem or problems that initially lead us to the use of drugs, alcohol, or other destructive behaviors. Again, I am speaking from a personal perspective and don't claim to be a psychologist, counselor or involved in any other medical profession. This is an account of my life experiences and these experiences have taught me valuable lessons that I would never have learned simply by counseling or the reading of material. Don't get me wrong though, there are some instances where people do need that sort of attention and I would recommend that they do seek the help needed for their situation.

Back to the story in Matthews about the spirit that leaves a man only to return with seven more unclean spirits. When we become sober, we appear to be clean and swept on the outside, yet there's no new life inside, leaving the opportunity for the unclean spirit to return and do more damage to our lives than at first. Now if we were true to ourselves I'm sure that I'm not alone in saying that drugs were not our only issues! There are so many substitutes that take over the place of our addictions and we claim victory over just one area of our lives; yet still have a list of other things wrong within ourselves.

When we come to the Lord, life takes on new meaning and we don't have to acknowledge continually of what the Lord has already paid the price for.

What am I saying? When we confess that we are still addicts/alcoholics even though we've been sober for a number of years, we are admitting the possibility of those unclean spirits to re-enter into our lives. That admission causes us to walk in fear and fear causes torment. "Once an addict, always an addict" is a slogan often rehearsed by members of the AA/CA/NA originations that actually allows a person to remain in the state of emptiness mentioned in Matthews. Now to me, that's mental agony. Why constantly proclaim something and walk in fear of something that no longer exists in your life. Although you may not be complete in your deliverance, you make the first step when you acknowledge that you do have a problem, yet also acknowledge that there is a way out called deliverance through Jesus Christ. **John 8:36** says; "If the Son therefore shall make you free, ye shall be free indeed."

As a Christian we believe in the word of God, which says, "God doesn't give us the spirit of fear, but of Power, Love and of a Sound mind." **II Timothy 1:7**.

That doesn't mean you won't be tempted. It doesn't mean you won't fall back into your old habit of using. It does however mean that through your temptation, God will make a way of escape so you won't give in. See: **I Corinthians 10:13.**

One of the things I had to come to grips with as a new Christian was what the Bible said; "Therefore if any man be in Christ, he is a new creature: old things are passed away; behold, all things are become new." **2 Corinthians 5:17**. I have found this to be a progressive attitude. It wasn't something that became automatic with me. Throughout the first years of being saved, or a new creature, I had to come to grips with a truth! I had an old self! An old nature! That old self wanted to live life like I wanted to live, or at least how I thought I wanted to live. The old self was selfish in all respect of the word, because I just wanted what I wanted, when I wanted it and the way I wanted it. I sought the things of the world to appease me for comfort and satisfaction. Had nice places to live, good jobs, women, all the comforts of life; or so I thought anyway.

On the flip side of the old life; Christ offers a new life through the Spirit of God. This new life begins as we repent of our sins and confess Jesus Christ as our Lord and Savior. Water Baptism is also symbolic to our new life as it is an outward expression of an inward change by full submersion in water, symbolizing the death, burial and resurrection of Jesus Christ. Again, this doesn't make us perfect, but it starts us on our way.

Unlike someone who is without Christ in their life, Jesus made provisions for the believer in **1 John 1:9**; "If we confess our sins, He is faithful and just to forgive us our sins, and to cleanse us from all unrighteousness." Life in Christ has it's benefits, but we're not to take those benefits for granted and abuse the privilege we have as being children of God.

If you do fall back into your addiction remember these words in **Proverbs 24:16:** "For a just man falls seven times, and rises up again...." The verse simply means you're human and as humans we tend to make bad choices in life which will lead us to carry out old habits.

When I reflected on the many times that I stumbled back onto drugs, I really didn't understand why at first. "I know I'm saved, but why do I keep doing the same thing over and over and over again?" I kept asking myself "Why do I keep making these choices to fall back into sin? Am I really an addict until I die?"

Fortunately, I learned I didn't have to own up to that fact, once I understood that the first time I gave my life to the Lord, I took on being a new creature in Christ. I was born again as a brand new baby. I don't know many babies running around making decisions for themselves, do you? As a new babe in Christ, I had received the Holy Spirit. Like any baby, I had to be nurtured inside. Often times than not the first things we want to do after a little while of being sober is to go out and buy a nice car or array ourselves in jewelry and nice clothes, giving an outward show of what we call success. But Jesus called the scribes and Pharisees of His day "Hypocrites!" "For ye make clean the outside of the cup and of the platter, but within they are full of extortion and excess." It begins with the inward part and exudes outwardly. Somehow society has gotten things wrong! But there is a remedy!

How is that done? You confess Jesus Christ as your Lord and Savior and repent of your sins. Afterwards, you might want to get baptized with water, just as Christ did as an example to us **Matthew 3:13-15**.

In the book of **John 3:5,** Jesus tells a man named Nicodemus that he must be born of water and Spirit or else he will not enter the Kingdom of God. Yeah I know; that confused me a little at first, too. One day, the Lord revealed the meaning to me.

When John the Baptist baptized Jesus, he was showing us how to display a change in our lives by an outward expression. In **Matthew 3:16** it says: "And Jesus, when He was baptized, went up straightway out of the water: and, lo, the heavens were opened unto Him, and He saw the Spirit of God descending like a dove, and lighting or landing, upon Him...."

It's not that dramatic today, but the Spirit of God does come into every believer's heart. At that point, we are newly born in Christ, because the Spirit of God dwells inside of us.

This begins our conception into a new birth and life with Christ, now comes the part where we grow into maturity.

How do we grow to maturity so we don't fall back into using, or just sinning again? The Bible says in **Galatians 5:16** that "If you walk in the Spirit, you shall not fulfill the lust of the flesh." In the book of **James 1:14, 15** it says: "But every man is tempted, when he is drawn away of **his own lust**, and enticed, then when lust has conceived, it brings forth sin: and sin, when it is finished, brings forth death." "For the wages (earnings) of sin is death; but the gift of God is eternal life through Jesus Christ our Lord." **Romans 6:23**

The programs of AA/NA/CA are not bad support groups, they have been around since the 1800's and have managed to help millions remain sober, but the concept makes them vulnerable to compromise of the word of God. After talking with quite a few faithful members of the AA/NA/CA groups, being personally involved in the meetings and researching the origins of AA, I've noticed a certain allegiance to their doctrine, which means teachings.

It actually started with a society called the "Washington Temperance Movement" and later became the "The Oxford Group," founded in 1908. It was also called; "A First Century Christian Fellowship." In 1934 Bill W., founder of, "The Big Book," was introduced to the group, which based the concept of their belief in Jesus Christ as, "The Great Physician" Who was able to deliver him from alcoholism. (Early History of Alcoholics Anonymous; by Mitchell K.)

But throughout the years, the most important factor is being ignored. That factor is Jesus Christ Himself. **I John 2:23** says: "Whoever denies the Son does not have the Father; he who acknowledges the Son has the Father also." I have found that most groups within these organizations admit to "A god of their under-standing" but never acknowledge Jesus as Lord! This in itself is an error of what Bill W. himself had estab-lished within the ranks of this organization.

Disclaimer: This book is not intended to infringe upon the practice of AA/NA/CA fellowship, nor is its pri-mary focus intended towards AA/NA/CA; the intend-ed focus is however to inform everyone, regardless of their bondage, that deliverance of any kind is possible through Jesus Christ and Him alone.

Proverbs 14:12; "There is a way that seems right to a man, But the end of those ways are the ways of death (spiritual separation from God) or could lead to the physical death as well, without Christ in your life.

Knowing who we are in Christ gives us the victory over our own thoughts, feelings, beliefs and limitations in life. Seeking God through Jesus Christ is the only way we will find and experience true life and deliverance. This leads us to the first step; **Acknowledge;**

> **Note:** These are the basic steps necessary to take in relation to ones walk as a Christian, and available to all who will accept Christ into their lives. Christ came to set the captives free, and the time of deliverance is totally de-pendent on God and your sincere desire, and willingness to be set free.

2 | Step 1: Acknowledge

I was blessed to grow up in a home with three brothers and three sisters. To make ends meet mom worked as a nurse during the week. She married when I was too young to know what was going on at the time. I believe I was about five or six years old then. In fact, I remember being at her wedding at my grandmother's house when I asked someone, "Who is that man with mommy"? Remember, I was only five at the time!

Because my mother worked during the week, we stayed with our grandparents where we would also attend school. We went home on the weekends. It was at my grandparents house that I began to hear things mentioned about God. My grandmother used to work around the house doing laundry, cooking, and washing dishes. All the while, she sang songs like "Jesus loves me this I know…" and "Amazing grace, how sweet the sound." I didn't understand everything, but I knew that there was a connection between the songs my grandmother sang and our participation, usually unwillingly, in church each Sunday. I left church when I became old enough to make decisions for myself and didn't really return until I was thirty six years old. It wasn't until much later in life that these songs became more meaningful to me.

Over the years of absents from church I realized that something wasn't right in my life. It was during the progression of years of drinking, drugging, womanizing etc; that my first real encounter with what I thought to be a Christian took place. That is outside of my grandparents' life. I met this guy at work one day, his name was Ryan. There was something different in the way Ryan talked and carried himself. Nothing ever seemed to bother Ryan. He seemed to be always at peace. I was living in Columbus, Ohio at the time. As I mentioned in the first chapter, I did hold some pretty good jobs during my addictions and of course it was dully for the purposes of supporting my additions.

After some time of casually observing Ryan, curiosity got the best of me, and I asked him why nothing seemed to bother him.

He began to talk with me about the Lord. He explained the effects of sin that had been passed down from Adam, and that we all have sinned and fallen short of the glory of the Lord.

Weeks went by and I would occasionally ask Ryan more about his Christ that gave him so much peace. He would cheerfully answer all of my questions, and I listened intently to everything that he was saying to me because I wanted that peace for myself.

As time went on he invited me to his church. It took a few weeks but then I reluctantly accepted! I believe now that I look back in hindsight, that I was a little apprehensive about going because I was somewhat of an introvert and I knew from growing up that everybody that's in church, isn't so sympathetic about your problems and situation in life. I feared of being prejudged by others who I knew could not possibly relate to what I had experienced in life up to that point. After setting those fears aside I told him that I would come and visit, and that was all that I intended to do! I was pretty emphatic about that, or so I thought.

That next Sunday, I went to Ryan's church. I sat there looking around asking myself "why am I here"? "these people are crazy"! is one of the many thoughts going through my mind at the time. Then my attention went to the pastor and his sermon was so much related to something I was going through at that time. I instantly became upset with my friend Ryan and began to wonder, "Did Ryan mention something to him about me"? "How does he know that about me"? I thought that way because I had talked to Ryan quite a bit about some of the things I was experiencing in life. I felt betrayed as the pastor continued to talk and by the previous experiences I had when I was younger in church, this didn't leave me with a good impression. I buried my suspicions about Ryan's betrayal, or so I thought, that day. I was so convicted by what was being said that by the end of that message the pastor gave, I was in tears. By the end of the service, I not only gave my life to the Lord, but joined the church as well.

Later in life I found out how the Lord reaches you through other people, and reveals things to us by His Spirit. I was able to forgive Ryan of what I just knew was betrayal.

In order for you to understand some things in my life, I have to take you back some 15 years before I got saved, and some years after I got saved as well. I was thirty six years old when I got saved.

I got involved in drugs and alcohol in my teen years. I started drinking wine and beer at a very young age. I believe I was about thirteen or fourteen years old when I started drinking. I did it because of peer pressure, trying to hang out with the crowd. I never got used to the taste of alcohol; even though I was consuming twenty four packs of beer a day by the time I was twenty. As the years progressed, so did my appetite for drugs and everything acquainted with it. My life began to spiral downward and didn't even realize it because I thought in my mind that I was enjoying life. During this progression I married four times, and had eight children out of three of the four marriages. I wasn't in their lives like I hoped because by then, the world had such a grip on my life and wasn't letting go.

The Bible says in **I John 2:16 that** "All that is in the world, the lust of the flesh, the lust of the eyes, and the pride of life, is not of the Father but is of the world." This brought me to the acknowledging of my sinfulness and the many lustful desires I had in life.

It took great pains for me to **acknowledge** my own weaknesses and come to the truth that I was spiritually bankrupt, separated from God and desperately needing some help. Yes, I was lost. In despair of being healed of my sickness, drugs and whatever else was keeping me from living life.

My life's journey and the choices I made landed me in a state penal institution for a year at the age of fifty. I never would have thought for an instant that I would be locked away in some prison at that age, although I had, in more instances than I care to remember, been in several city jails by then. Even more shocking to me, that's where I celebrated my fiftieth birthday. But the way I was drugging and gratifying other lustful desires, I knew incarceration was a divine plan of God. It was God's way of getting my attention. Nothing else made much sense because I had been saved for at least fourteen years by then.

I was making all the wrong decisions, pretty much

based on feelings, which led to the same results. The insanity had to stop, but how? I thought I was doing what I was supposed to be doing; or had I been?

Through it all, I didn't give up on getting to know the Lord. I would still attend church, Bible studies, yet I would still continue to do the things that I was not comfortable about doing anymore. Something inside of me would always tell me not to give up though. After all, I had seen something in my friend Ryan that I wanted to experience in my own life. That alone was an encouragement to me. As I continued to read the Bible and seek God, He began to reveal Himself to me more and more. I'm finding that God loves me in a way that doesn't make any human sense at all! He looks past our faults and shortcomings and sees our need for a Savior. He offers us His Son as our Savior so we can find peace in our lives today.

Later in my walk with the Lord I learned more about Adam and his purpose here on earth. The Bible says that the first Adam was made a living soul and the last Adam (Jesus) a quickening (life giving) spirit. **I Corinthians 15:45**

Initially man was made in the image of God. That means we had taken on the character of God; Love, Joy, Peace, Longsuffering, Kindness, Goodness, Faithfulness, Gentleness, and Self-Control: You can find that in **Galatians 5:22** Known as the "Fruit of the Spirit."

Adam was the first man who became a living soul. God breathed life into his nostrils. Adam transgressed against the law of God by eating of the fruit of the tree of the knowledge of good and evil which the Bible said that Eve, his wife gave him after she had taken of the fruit and did eat. This disobedience caused succeeding generations to be spiritually separated from God. This separation is what caused us to be born into sin. Adam was a type of Him (Jesus) who was to come and bear our sins, so that we may have a chance to be redeemed (brought back) into a right relationship with God and given the chance to take on a new life in Christ.

Like Jesus, Adam had authority over everything God created. But as man would have it, time and time again we disobey God's commands, causing us to be separated from fellowship with God. But God had a plan of redemption from the beginning of time. It was the gift of His Son, Jesus Christ predestined before the beginning of the world, because God knew what was in man's heart. Even from the very beginning of Adams fall God was preparing the way for Jesus, and God used the sacrifice of an animal to cover Adam and Eve after their sin in Genesis 3:21 as an example of God's covering grace (gift) by the shedding of blood which would ultimately be done finally and sufficiently by Jesus Christ.

Accepting the gift isn't easy for anyone. It certainly wasn't easy for me. Even though I had been saved, I had to realize something just wasn't right in my own life. I had to **acknowledge** that I'm first and foremost, a sinner separated from God in relationship. I had to **acknowledge** that without Christ in my life, I would be eternally lost, with no hope of ever receiving His peace that surpasses all understanding. Without Christ, how would I be "More than a conquer" and walk in true deliverance and victory!

It was a difficult thing to grasp, the shedding of blood! Just the thought of it made me cringe but after coming into a more understanding of why blood had to be shed I could fully understand and appreciate the purpose of it in long range. Without it we would be eternally lost. Our sins would never be done away with and we would never be able to experience the peace that only God Himself can provide.

In **John 14:27** Jesus says; "Peace I leave with you, My peace I give unto you: not as the world giveth, give I unto you. Let not your heart be troubled, neither let it be afraid."

We must believe that God, through Jesus Christ will give us this peace that the world cannot give us. The peace that the world offers is contingent on our possessions, and like our possessions will fade, so will our temporary peace.

With Christ, "All things are possible, for them that Believe…." This takes us to the next step:

3

Step 2: Believe

"Let not your heart be troubled: you **believe** in God, **believe** also in Me (Jesus)." **John 14:1.** Jesus spoke these words in the gospel of John. The question that I often get, and that I myself had a problem with was, "How can you believe in someone you can't see"? Some believe in many gods, but as a Christian, we believe that there is only one true and living God. His name is Jehovah… amongst other names that express His sovereignty, deity, and holiness in the Holy Bible.

My grandmother used to tell us about this God and how He watches over us and provides for our needs. She said He was always present, but I'd never seen Him, which naturally created some doubt in my life.

I remember when I was five or six years old, my grandmother used to take me to Pittsburgh, PA to see a lady named Kathryn Kuhlman. I knew then that there was something special about that lady. People used to go up to the stage where she was and she would always pray that God would heal these people and people did get healed! I thought that was amazing, but my grandmother would always tell me that it was the power of God, working through Kathryn Kuhlman, that healed the people.

One time, Kathryn Kuhlman talked about the power of God touching someone in the rafters. It seemed as if she was pointing directly at me as she was talking, and I started feeling this heat come over me. It was so intense I began to break out in a sweat. My grandmother looked at me with amazement and said, "Your face is just shining"! At the time I didn't know what was going on but; now I know the glory of the Lord was shining on my face as was the glory shined on Moses' face when he came down from Mt. Sinai with the Ten Commandments. **See Exodus 34:35** There is something about being in the presence of God, even when we don't know it, that leaves an impression that maybe we can't see within ourselves, but revealed to others.

Throughout the years, God revealed Himself in many circumstances in my life. He protected me, provided for me and kept me from all evil, or at least the consequences of the evil choices I made for myself in life. As I am growing more mature in the Lord, I'm learning that there is a God that does all the things my grandmother talked about. I've learned to trust in that God which once belonged to my grandmother, and that I had seen in my friend Ryan as well. I think about the meeting of the Samaritan woman who met Jesus at the well mentioned in the gospel of John chapter 4. After Jesus told the woman all about her life, she went into the town and told everyone to "come and see a man that told me everything I ever did"! In verse 42, after hearing Jesus for themselves, the towns' people responded; "Now we believe, not because of thy saying: for we have heard Him ourselves, and know that this is indeed the Christ, the Savior of the world." As I pray, study and practice His word out in my own life, He reveals Himself and His purpose for my life. He will do the same for you, if you welcome Him into your life and humble yourself to Him, and believe that He's able to do all things but fail.

This God whom my grandmother knew has become the God that I know and **believe** in through a personal relationship through His Son, Jesus Christ and by the administration of the Holy Spirit, Who was sent to live in all believers that the possibility of living a new life would be made possible.

Often times, our unbelief restricts God from revealing Himself to us. **Hebrews 11:6**; "But without faith it is impossible to please Him (God): for he that comes to God must **believe** that He is, and that He is a rewarder of them that diligently seek Him."

Believing that God sent His only begotten son as a

living sacrifice for our sins is the beginning of true life. Believing that Jesus sent the Holy Spirit is the beginning of a relationship with God. It is only through Jesus, by the empowerment of the Spirit of God that enables us to even begin to walk a new life. It's only through the Spirit of God that we can begin to understand God's Word and know His will for our lives.

You know, I used to read the Bible like it was just a good storybook. I didn't know that it was a pattern of life that we as Christians should live by. When that reality hit me, I began to change my reading habits and started applying the word that God speaks through the Bible to my own life. As a result, my life is changing. The book of **James 1:22** says; "But be ye doers of the word, and not hearers only, deceiving your own selves."

We often attempt to incorporate our own understanding into God's word, but **Proverbs 3:5,6** cautions us to; "Trust in the Lord with all our heart and lean not to our own understanding, in all our ways acknowledge Him and He will direct our Path." Setting up our own carnal structures, patterns and institutions may have admirable intentions, but it always ends up with carnal results. It's the same as mixing water with oil: it just doesn't work. **Proverbs 14:12** tells us; "There is a way which seemeth right unto a man, but the end thereof are the ways of death." Simply meaning, if we attempt to do things our way, outside of how God instructs us to do them, we do it in vain and have no future with Him in eternity. We will remain spiritually dead, and eventually eternally without God.

I Corinthians 2:13 says, "The Holy Spirit teaches, comparing spiritual things with spiritual." And it's only by God's Spirit in us that we can be identified as belonging to God. **Romans 8:16**; "The Spirit Himself bears witness with our spirit that we are the children of God."

When we come to believe in a power greater than ourselves that can deliver us from bondage, I think it wise to know and believe in the only true living God who created the heavens and the earth and all that dwells within. Don't you? He gives us the power and authority over the entire world and all that's within it by His Spirit and through His Son Jesus Christ. After all, if we were created in his image, don't you think he knows what's best for our lives? When we believe in who God is, we can believe God for everything else.

God is above all, He is Sovereign and there is none like Him in all the earth, or universe for that matter. We can't even begin to know God in His person, only what He reveals to us will we ever know. **Isaiah 55:8, 9** says; "For my thoughts are not your thoughts, nor are your ways my ways, for as the heavens are higher than the earth, so are my ways higher than your ways, and my thoughts than your thoughts." Read **Isaiah 55:10, 11** as well: "Gods word never returns void." Simply saying that God is beyond any natural comprehension, He is the Alpha and the Omega, the Beginning and the End, Which means that He alone knows the outcome of all things. We are only to trust Him in the process between the now and eternity. We often quote **Romans 8:28;** "All things work together for good…," but do we really apply the second part of that verse, "to those who love Him, and who are the called....."? Believing goes beyond our natural belief system. It extends to how we respond to what we believe and our actions in whom we place our trust. It's easy to say "we believe" as long as things are going good for us; but what about when things are going not so good! Do we still hold to the belief that "All things work together for good"?

So believing is so much more than just professing that you believe, but it's also acting upon what or who we believe in. It takes the practice of doing what God says according to the Word of God, living it out in our lives, once we ourselves have accepted Jesus into our lives and allow the Holy Spirit to give us direction that is. It's not easy by any means; none the less rewarding. **1Peter 5:10** tells us; "But the God of all grace, who hath called us unto His eternal glory by Christ Jesus, after that ye have suffered a while, make you perfect (mature), establish, strengthen, settle you." I believe that God arraigned this process just to see how committed we would be! Just to see if we're going to stand through the test of time. It certainly has been challenging for me to say the least! And not to get myself discouraged, I do know as long as I remain on this earth, test will come. God has given me victory time and time again through my troubles and I know He will continue to provide His divine protection and guidance for my life as long as I continue to believe on Him and the finished work on Calvary through Jesus Christ. Suffering for righteousness sake is a suffering that is acceptable to God. The bible says that if we suffer for something we've done outside of what God tells us, what reward do we have? **See 1 Peter 3:13, 14**

4

Step 3: Confess

In the first two chapters, we've learned how to acknowledge that we are sinners, and believe that God has sent Jesus Christ, His Son, to save us from the wages or penalties of our sins by sacrificing His life for ours. This third step of confession comes at the point of change in our lives. Before I go any further I would like to say that it does matter to whom we are confessing. Let me say that again, **IT MATTERS TO WHOM WE ARE CONFESSING OURS SINS TO**!

Romans 10:9 says: "If you confess with your mouth the Lord Jesus and believe in your heart that God has raised Him from the dead, you will be saved." **Verse 10** goes on to say: "For with the heart man believes unto righteousness; and with the mouth confession is made unto salvation." This is done through prayer, either lead by someone who knows the Lord, or in the privacy of your own closet, metaphorically speaking. I believe the whole idea is that when you do confess, that you know with certainty who you are confessing to and for what reason the confession is being made. Confessing that you are a sinner and confessing that only Jesus can wipe your sins away are both vital in the beginning of your new life with Christ.

There is also an outward confession of our faith which is called the Baptism of Repentance. In the gospel of John it mentions the person of John the Baptist, who was called to be the forerunner for Jesus, "The voice of one crying in the wilderness, Prepare ye the way of the Lord, make His paths straight." He baptized with the baptism of repentance and this confession was made by a total submersion in water, symbolizing the death, burial and resurrection of Jesus Christ. It's also the beginning of a new life as a Christian, a recovered life of which satan had stolen from Adam, or that Adam relinquished, depending on your viewpoint, in the garden of Eden, that allowed all to be born in sin and separated from God. What comes after the water baptism puts the seal to being in a new relationship. That seal being of the Holy Spirit.

In the book of Acts the second chapter verse 38, Peter answers a question posed by the response of the crowed which Peter just preached to; "What shall we do?" Peters' response was; "Repent, (change your mind of the lifestyle you've been living) and be baptized every one of you in the name of Jesus

Christ for the remission (to be released from or set free) of sins, and ye shall receive the gift of the Holy Ghost."

Some may ask the question; why do we need to go through all that? Remember, "We were born in sin, shaped into iniquity." To recover in the biblical since means to return to a preexistent condition. This condition preexisted in the Garden of Eden thousands of years ago after the creation of all things by God. When we as Christians say that we're in recovery, we're actually saying we're in the process of a significant change in our lives, other than the fact that we're no longer drinking or drugging. This recovery takes us back before the fall in the Garden of Eden just after Adam was formed and before he sinned against God. We are separated from God, without Jesus Christ as Lord and Savior of our lives, but in the process of our recovery, we are being reconciled to God through our relationship with Jesus Christ. But I've come to realize that it's not just about me being reconciled to God. The Bible tells us that; "All things are of God, who hath reconciled us to Himself by Jesus Christ, and hath given to us the ministry of reconciliation." **2 Corinthians 5:18**.

This doesn't bring about an immediate change for some. I am an example of how long change can take and how longsuffering God is towards us! Even after I visited my friends' church and was baptized, I remained addicted for years following. My addiction didn't mean I wasn't saved. It did mean God needed to deliver me from my sins as we carry a multitude of them without even being aware of them. There were things so deeply imbedded within me, some things took time for even me to be made aware of. Things have a tendency to become complacent in our lives and can go on for years without our knowledge of it even existing in our lives, which is why sometimes it may be a good idea to listen to positive criticism, and I do mean positive. Growing up I faced allot of negative criticism, even in the church! Often, I had to encourage myself in the Lord as King David found himself doing on various occasions. Remember, Christ came to bear the penalty of our sinfulness, but that sin nature will continue until the Holy Spirit cleanses us; or until Christ returns and we put on our celestial (heavenly) bodies. The Bible also tells us that the flesh is always warring against the spirit. That's a constant struggle going on within us. **Read James 1:15, 16** when you get the chance.

Romans 6:4 says; "Therefore we were buried with Him through baptism into death, that just as Christ was raised from the dead by the glory of the Father, even so we also should walk in newness of life."

When we walk in newness of life, it would mean that we would have to rid ourselves of old habits, ways and behaviors. This involves a continuous confession of where we are in life at that particular time and that change in our own behavior is needed.

Often times this step takes awhile, especially if you are as stubborn to change or advice as I was. Confession implies that we know what we're confessing to! Sometimes it takes someone else to point out things in our lives that we can't see within ourselves that may not be right. Or the Holy Spirit will reveal those things to us. Either way we have been practicing these behaviors for so long, they become as naturally a part of our lives as our limbs: fingers, toes, eyes, etc; When God reveals these character defects, he gives us the tools and ability to change them. For a Christian, change is not an option. It's inevitable. You'll find throughout the New Testament places where it tells us to take off the old man or nature that caters to the flesh; and put on the new man or regenerate man born after the Spirit which focuses in on living the life that God has intended for us to live.

Even though it's been some time since I was delivered from drugs, I still find myself confessing my sins to God, in thought mostly, or maybe in things that I say or do that displeases God, allowing Him to place His character within me, and removing anything or anyone that's offensive to Him from my life. Sometimes that comes with the territory!

II Corinthians 13:5 says; "Examine yourselves, whether you are in the faith; prove your own selves. Know you not your own selves, how that Jesus Christ is in you, except you be reprobates"? Nelson's Bible Dictionary defines reprobate as "One who fails a test and is rejected." In this case, that person is rejected by God because that person would continually and intentionally sin against God and not seek forgiveness or conviction for themselves. This would nullify any hope of salvation through Jesus Christ. **Ezekiel 18:4** says: "Behold, all souls are mine; as the soul of the father, so also the soul of the son is mine: the soul that sins, it shall die."

The process of continually confessing my sins made me look at that word, "reprobate." I looked a little closer into that word because I started to get a little concerned, or a better word for what I felt was convicted. I used to pray; "Lord, don't let me be a reprobate." I didn't want to miss out on God for any reason, but I just couldn't bring myself to stop committing the acts of sin. After I prayed and studied persistently, God began to open my eyes. I read in **Hebrews 4:15;** "For we have not an high priest which cannot be touched with the feeling of our infirmities; but was in all points tempted like as we are, yet without sin." In **Romans 8:6** it said; "To be carnally minded is death; but to be spiritually minded is life and peace." And I found in **verse 13** "For if you live after the flesh, you shall die; but if you through the Spirit do mortify the deeds of the body, you shall live." Finally, I was lead to Galatians **5:16** "Walk in the Spirit, and you shall not fulfill the lust of the flesh."

As God continued to reveal Himself, I was able to apply His word to my life. I got the victory over the many obstacles and challenges that I encountered, giving me the ability to trust in Him for the victory in my battles ahead. I was given closure by God of just what being a reprobate meant and a clearer understanding of the grace that God had shown me throughout the years of my continual fallings. If I were to continually and intentionally keep sinning against God, with no conviction at all, then God would turn me over to a reprobate mind. The key word was "intentionally." Each time I sinned, I cried out to the Lord for forgiveness, and as I continued to strengthen my relationship with Him, my cries became more and more deep and sincere. I couldn't then, and I still can't now, even phantom the kind of love that God had shown me in my natural mind, but then again, God is all but natural!

James 5:16 urges us to "Confess your faults one to another, and pray one for another, that you may be healed. The effectual fervent prayer of a righteous man avails much." It's difficult for men to show emotions sometimes, not to mention share them with others, for fear of being considered weak. But the Bible is clear! As a Christian, you must not only confess, but pray for others, that **YOU** may be healed. Focusing on others actually helps our personal growth with the Lord. Word of caution! Be prayerful about what you're confessing and to whom you are confessing to! The reality is that some people have other motives and may use what you say to harm you with what you're confiding in them about; while on the other hand, confessing our sins should be done through Jesus Christ to God, Who alone can not only forgive us our sins, but cleanse us from all unrighteousness. Confessing your fault as **Matthew 5:23, 24** implies is to make amends with whomever has differences with you! So confession covers a wide area and includes every relationship you can think of. Our relationship with God first and foremost, our relationship with each other and with ourselves! When we begin to get honest with ourselves and acknowledge the sin state that we're in, then and only then can we begin to allow God to deliver us from ourselves, heal us, restore and then reveal His purpose and plan for us individually and corporately as well. Confession clears the way for God to have full course in our lives. It will give us hope where we were once hopeless.

Confession leads us to the next step: repenting

5

Step 4: Repent

When you hear the word "**Repent**" what crosses your mind? It will probably be the same thing that first entered mine! "What does repent mean?" For years to follow after I was saved I thought it to be a sorrowful feeling or regret for doing something wrong. Once the feeling passed, I was back doing just what I did before. I thought it to be regret for blowing all my money, not having anything to eat, no money left over to do much of anything other than wait on the next time I would have money in my hands, just to do it all over again. Somebody knows what I'm talking about!

That was my story anyway. I thought I had a reprobate mind because I would do the same thing over and over. As I continued seeking God, I found I'd been committing a certain sin for so long, I didn't know any other way to live. It was a way of life for me, or so I was lead to believe by the thoughts I allowed in my mind.

But God showed me that true repentance meant changing my thoughts, behaviors and deeds. It's an exercise! Just as consistent exercise produces positive results, so does the exercise of repenting and changing our thoughts to how God knows things should be done, and then doing it. When my thinking changed, my actions began to change. When my actions changed, the way I lived began to change.

Some may say that this part of repentance is an easy thing to do, but it's not. I asked myself repeatedly, "How can you stop doing what you're so accustomed to doing for practically all of your life"? Finally, I asked God to show me how to change. Through a lot of prayer, study and commitment of God's word, through trials and self-denial of self gratification, God has and is showing me what it is to have a repentant heart.

I mentioned the word exercise in repentance because that's just what it takes. I like to look up the definitions of words that will help me better understand things so I looked up the word exercise. It is defined as "bodily or mental exertion, something performed as a means of practice, or a putting into action or effect." (dictionary.com) Each definition shows a pattern - that there is work and effort involved, and it all leads to the achievement of something. The Bible says in **Romans 6:16**, "Know ye not, that to whom ye yield yourselves servants to obey, his servants ye are to whom ye obey; whether of sin unto death, or of obedience unto righteousness"? Simply put, if we exercise fulfilling our fleshly desires all the time, our results will be self gratification, which is sin, which will lead to death (spiritual separation from God), but could also lead to the physical death as well! The flip side of that is that if we exercise ourselves to godliness, we'll have all things that God wants to and will supply us with! **1 Timothy 4:8** says; "For bodily exercise profits little: but godliness is profitable unto all things, having promise of the life that now is, and of that which is to come." Although this verse is talking about abstaining from sexual activities while fasting or physical exercise, it also mentions the long term results of exercising our spirits to godliness having promises of life now, and the life hereafter.

In the book of Hebrews the eleventh chapter it talks about Moses choosing to suffer affliction with the people of God, than to enjoy the pleasures of sin for a season. While we exercise our sinful pleasures it makes us feel good, for a season. It's not lasting! Same as when we physically work out! It feels good for a while, it could be years that we enjoy the physique, but then we grow old and the muscle turns to flab! Does that sound like anyone we know? When we understand God's perspective of life, "A day is as a thousand years; and a thousand years as a day" **2 Peter 3:8,** we can understand the vanity of continuing in our sins, thinking we're going to get lasting pleasures in them. Repentance offers us the opportunity to change the direction in life from what we're accustomed to, and turn to God and apply His principles to our lives.

The Bible says that; "The Lust of the eye, Lust of the flesh and the Pride of Life" is of the world and these are the very things that lead us to committing the acts of sins and walking contrary to what God would have us to walk. **I John 2:16**

Those verses are why I say we are not recovering from anything, but we are being shaped into new creatures; recovering to something, our original state of being as in the Garden of Eden. "Therefore if any man be in Christ, he is a new creature; old things are passed away; behold, all things are become new," **II Corinthians 5:17.** To repent and become a child of God means to be born again and take on a totally new direction in life!

I had to repent about many areas in my life. But after I'd repented, I had to replace my thoughts and plans with something else. As a Christian, my responsibility was and is to replace what I've known through life's experiences with what God tells me in His word, the Bible. There is no other way that the right change can come about unless it's through God's Word!

John 14:6 Jesus said that "I am the way, the truth,

and the life: no man comes to the Father, but by Me." That alone leaves no room for any other means of salvation or eternal life. Jesus paid it all and all to Him I owe.

6

Step 5: Pray

What is prayer? It's communication with God. Some would believe in our daily lives that communications with each other is simply "I'm talking so you need to listen." Not so! Communication is not only talking, but listening effectively. More importantly, it's listening to the voice of God.

There are many ways that God uses to speak to the believer. He speaks through the Bible, true, but He also speaks through other people as well. He may also speak to us through our circumstances. However He chooses to speak to us we need to be in the position to not only hear, but recognize His voice when He speaks. There are allot of voices out here trying to tell you "this is the way to live" but if it doesn't line up with what God's Word is saying, I would have a real problem with that. In **John 10:27** Jesus is saying; "My sheep hear my voice, and I know them, and they follow me." You see, that is a mystery to most, and it will remain a mystery to many, that is if we don't plug into who we really are. God made all men in His image and He knows each and everyone of us, even before our physical bodies entered this world! **2 Timothy2:19** says; "Never the less the foundation of God stands sure, having this seal, The Lord knows them that are His, And, let everyone that names the name of Christ depart from iniquity (unrighteousness, lawlessness) When I look back, I see how other people were vital influences in my life carrying God's message in their lifestyles. Then there were others who preached a good message, but the lifestyle didn't add up with the message! Not judging that person, but only making reference to those who walk after Christ; as opposed to those who say they walk after Christ. The Bible says that "we will know them by their fruits." **See Matthew 7:15 – 20.** The fruits that relate to this portion of scripture is found in the character of a person and not just mere outward performance. It exudes from the inside out just as my friend Ryan demonstrated his fruit just by reflecting peace in his life and then when he invited me to his church, that's called discipling. The pastor was a channel of the Holy Ghost while preaching his sermon and it reflected on a situation I was personally experiencing at the time.

God's message comes through unexpected means, but you'll know He's speaking because He will also confirm His word. **II Corinthians 13:1** says; "This is the third time I am coming to you. In the mouth of two or three witnesses shall every word be established."

God knows what's best for us. It is only through Jesus Christ that we will receive anything from Him, anything good that is. We can obtain things in life and be the most miserable with them! Somehow the church has drifted away from the real purpose of prayer. **James 4:1 – 3** in the NLT says; "What is causing the quarrels and fights among you? Don't they come from the evil desires at war within you? You want what you don't have, so you scheme and kill to get it. You are jealous of what others have, but you can't get it, so you fight and wage war to take it away from them. Yet you don't have what you want because you don't ask God for it. And even when you ask, you don't get it because your motives are all wrong-you want only what will give you pleasure." Communicating with God is not an option; it is a requirement. If you like to talk and be heard, stop now and listen to what God has to say.

Listening to the voice of God will help us overcome many obstacles in life. It will allow us to be more Christ like in living a godly life. It will sustain us as we encounter trials and troubles known as the storms of life.

We've been doing things our way for years and we have seen the results. **Proverbs 3:5, 6** says; "Trust in the Lord with all your heart; and lean not unto your own understanding. In **all** your ways acknowledge

Him, and He shall direct your paths." I put emphasis on the word **all** for a reason. Too many times, we don't want to acknowledge God in everything, only what appeases us. We don't want to relinquish control, even though he created everything, including us in His image and for His purpose. We are somewhat selective when it comes to the things of God.

Picking what we think applies to us and discarding what we think doesn't apply, doesn't work. We have to believe that **all** of God's Word is truth and applies to us all. I like Job's response to his wife after he lost everything he had and his wife insisted that he "curse God and die." Job replied; "What? Shall we receive good at the hand of God, and shall we not receive evil?" The NLT puts it this way; "Should we accept only good things from the hand of God and never anything bad"? **Job 2:10**. We only want to hear the blessings and favor of God; and not the judgment and wrath of God. God doesn't often times use His wrath to condemn us, but to correct us and save us from the sin we involve ourselves in. Not to destroy us, but to allow us to get it right before He returns for His church. The Bible says in **2 Peter 3:9**; "The Lord is not slack concerning His promise, as some men count slackness; but is longsuffering to us-ward, not willing that any should perish, but that all should come to repentance." This time that He's allowing us to get things right is called "grace" a dispensation of time that God is demonstrating His divine unmerited favor towards us. Through our prayers we communicate to

Him, for ourselves and each other. Our desire to do His will and prepare for His soon return for His church without spot or blemish should be our focal point in life. In our best attempt to do this ourselves would lead to certain destruction. In **Proverbs 14:12** it says; "There is a way that seems right unto a man, but the end thereof are the ways of death."

But the Bible says "acknowledge Him in **all** our ways, and He shall direct thy paths." **Proverbs 3:6**. **James 1:17** says "Every good gift and every perfect gift is from above, and comes down from the Father of lights, with whom is no variableness, neither shadow of turning." This would involve us praying according to God's will for our lives; not our will in wanting material possessions and allowing us to literally loose our souls! **Matthew 16:26** says; "For what is a man profited, if he shall gain the whole world, and lose his own soul? Or what shall a man give in exchange for his soul?" Now I must admit this didn't sound to pleasing to me at first because I had a knack for nice things! I had nice cars, nice apartment, nice women, well just keeping it real! But as I began to grow closer to the Lord in relationship I began to see things from another perspective. Solomon saw the same thing in Ecclesiastes. As wealthy as he was, as many wives as he had, as much power as he had, he finally saw that it was all vanity. His final summation was mentioned in the last verse of the book of **Ecclesiastes 12:13**; "Here now is my final conclusion: **Fear God and obey His commands**, for this is the whole duty of man." That fear Solomon was talking about is the fear of recognizing God in awe of Who He is, the Creator of all things, our provider, healer, warrior, Lord and King, etc;

Some count surrendering everything to Jehovah God as weakness. But if you humble yourself, God will restore His original promise. **Genesis 1:28** tells us to, "take back what the devil has stolen from you and reclaim your rightful ownership." **But we've got to do things God's way.**

The importance of prayer is stressed throughout the Bible. People of God have overcome great obstacles in life by praying, believing and acting on the commands of God. Trusting that God is able to do far more than we can ask; or think, allows Him to be all that He is in our lives both individually, and corporately as well.

I Thessalonians 5:17 tells us to "Pray without ceasing." When I first read this verse, I wondered, "Now how is that possible to pray all the time"? When I spent more time in prayer, I understood the verse to mean we must remain in tune with the Spirit of God by walking according to God's will for our lives meditating on His Word, constantly applying His Word to my life!

I've found in my own walk with the Lord that as I continue to stop looking at myself and keep my eyes on Jesus, that my desires to do and say the things I used to do and say became less and less important to me.

Pleasing God by seeking Him, not for material possessions, but for spiritual blessings such as peace, joy, love, kindness, goodness, faith, longsuffering, gentleness, meekness self control., has become my focus, and my reward will be eternal.

James 5:16; "Confess your trespasses to one another, and pray for one another, that you may be healed. The effective, fervent prayer of a righteous man avails much." **James 5:16.** This is where the importance of fellowship comes into play. I know that if there is anyone out there like I was, then you know how difficult it is to allow anyone to come into your circle, but as God would have it, that's just what's necessary in the body of Christ.

Hebrews 10:24,25 says; "And let us consider one another in order to stir up love and good works, **NOT** forsaking the assembling of ourselves together, as is the manner of some, but exhorting one another, and so much the more as you see the day approaching."

What is the approaching day? Read **Matthew 24:1-51** and you will see.

Prayer changes circumstances that ordinarily would have caused us to throw in the towel. God is a god of impossibilities. He is Jehova-Jireh, our provider, He is Jehova-rophe, our healer, He is Jehovah-nissi, our banner, He is Jehovah-M'Kaddesh, who sanctifies, He is Jehovah-shalom, our peace, He is Jehovah-tsidkenu, our righteousness, He is Jehovah-rohi, our Shepherd, He is Jehovah-shammah, and He is there.

He can make a way out of no way, but don't feel slighted if the route to deliverance is unexpected. He doesn't always give us what we want when we want it, but always gives us what we need at the right time. He knows we need it. I hope at this point in this book that we've all decided that we need a Savior. And His name is Jesus!

I wouldn't say that you should pray for material possessions, but for the blessings of God. **Jeremiah 29:11** says; "For I know the thoughts that I think toward you, says the Lord, thoughts of peace, and not of evil, to give you an expected end." Now this is where I struggled: "But seek first the kingdom of God, and His righteousness; and all these things shall be added to you." Growing up I always believed in possessing things was what made a person; but again, it's just the opposite when we become believers. Knowing that God is the supplier of all our needs, and that He only provides what is good for our well being, we do need to seek Him first and find out what He wants us to have. Things have a tendency to draw us away from God; and not to God. **Matthew 6:33. God needs believers who are totally submitted and surrendered to His will and purpose, those who have no want or need except what God has already ordained for them.** This doesn't mean that we shouldn't want things in life, but our first goal should be to doing the will of God. This is the proper order of things in God's eyes. As we just read how everything that is good comes from God, He gives them to us without changing or shifting from His promises.

I started receiving spiritual blessings only when I began to "Seek the Lord as for hidden treasure." He is now restoring my life through family relationships as well as opening numerous doors for ministry. This is just the beginning of a new life in God and I'm expecting so much more as I totally submit my will to God's will.

I can't stress the importance of prayer to you. God does answer prayer! I know and testify about the faithfulness of God in my life. Not just my own life either, but the lives of others, through submission others are being changed and renewed through prayer. He makes Himself available to us, if we but call upon His name with a sincere heart, and receive all that God has to offer us. "A man's heart devises his way; but the Lord directs his steps." **Proverbs 16:9.**

I do have to mention this next scripture because all too often I hear people talk about what God has blessed them with, and yes, the Bible does say that "it rains on the just as well as the unjust," but we have to be mindful that the enemy will give you gifts as well and we might think those things come from God. **Proverbs 15:29** says that; "The Lord is far from the wicked: but He heareth the prayer of the righteous."

There are many scriptures in the Bible that tells us of the proper way to approach a Holy God; and being wicked and continuing in our sins isn't one of them. He may answer a prayer while in those conditions, if we're seeking God for forgiveness of what we've done! His ears are always opened to the cries of repentance because He wants the best for us.

7

Step 6: Study

When I was a student in Junior High School and on to High School, studying wasn't one of my favorite past times. You couldn't get me to read a book. If no one was monitoring my work and if I didn't have someone looking over my shoulder, reading wouldn't have gotten done. The closest I got to a book was when I was reading a comic book, preferably Super Man comics. My grades were never up to par because I failed to study to prepare for the tests. It all seemed so trivial at the time. There were more important things to do in life, or so I thought at the time. I didn't realize just how much in life that I was really missing out on by not taking the time to read and study what I should have read. Life sure would have made more since to me growing up. As I grew older I started picking up books other than comics, but those books didn't require an awful lot of studying! Well, let's just say, there was nothing to study on that subject!

When I first began to read the Bible I almost slipped back into my lack of interest mode in not wanting to read because the language was of the King James language containing words like, thee and thou, shinneth, begat etc; which really made it difficult for me to focus any attention on my reading not alone studying the book. When I mentioned to someone about my lack of understanding of the Bible, they suggested that I pray before I read it and ask God for wisdom and understanding of His word, so I did! Of course my understanding didn't come over night, but I didn't give up because I found myself becoming enlightened to His Word! Of course as time went on I realized that God was revealing His Word to me as He willed it to be revealed. Typically it is a time passer to read a good book, or maybe to study a book for exams in school would be beneficial for everyday life to help you develop certain skills to make life a little easier. I have found that the Bible is so much more than that. During my younger years I used to hear the Bible referred to as an acronym: B.I.B.L.E, which meant: "Basic Instructions before Leaving Earth."

That didn't make any sense to me at the time. As I prayerfully began to read and study God's Word, I started noticing how the life in the Word of God began to transform my life! It dealt with many issues of life that we encounter on a daily basis, and not just this life but eternal life with God! When I started reading the book of James and ran across **James 1:22** where it says; "But be ye doers of the word, and not hearers only, deceiving your own selves," My eyes really began to open and my understanding deepening. In other words, the Bible was saying that what good is it if I just study the Bible and not put it into practice the things it was telling me to do! How to live and act as a Christian and live a life worthy of God was the focus. A new life like I've never experienced before has been introduced to me and I knew that what I was reading couldn't be achieved in my own intellect or ability. The life it was telling me I should live was next to impossible to me. This life was inconceivable! Later I learned, naturally, it was inconceivable in the natural sense, but with Christ, all things were possible. I knew a transformation had to take place in my life. That transformation had to come through the Spirit of God that was imparted in me at the time I gave my life to the Lord. It was at this point that I started to realize that "I am crucified with Christ: nevertheless I live; yet not I, but Christ liveth in me: and the life which I now live in the flesh I live by the faith of the Son of God, Who loved me, and gave Himself for me." God had given me a new life! Born of the Spirit of God! I began to realize the Christian's responsibility of studying the Word of God. **II Timothy 2:15** says to "Study to show thyself approved unto God, a workman that need not to be ashamed, rightly dividing the word of truth."

The inspired word of God is the key to all the necessities of life; nothing else gives as much fulfillment. **II Timothy 3:16** says that "All scripture is given by inspiration of God, and is profitable for doctrine, for reproof, for correction, for instruction in righteousness: **V.17**; that the man of God may be perfect (mature), thoroughly furnished unto all good works."

Deuteronomy 4:2 says: "You shall not add to the word which I command you, nor take from it, that you may keep the commandments of the Lord your God which I command you." This verse doesn't mean you can't read other books on the Christian faith, nor does it mean that you can't read various translations of the Bible. Instead, it warns against taking the scripture out of context, using it for your own personal interpretation. Some biblical translations do that, so I'd suggest that you pray that God would give you the discernment to choose the correct Bible to study. Too often I've seen people wanting to give their self interpretation of what the scripture says and the first thing I ask is; "Well, how often do you spend time with the Lord in prayer"? That's when I get the response; "Me and the Lord have our own relationship," or they give me some other off the wall response that tells me that they don't have a clue of who God is!

So true did the Lord say to Hosea in the book of **Hosea chapter 4:6**; "My people are destroyed for lack of knowledge......."

Proverbs 30:6: "Do not add to His words, lest He **rebuke** you, and you be found a liar."

God has inspired no other book that will lead us to

eternal life! Much literature purports to be by God, but is it? Here's how you can tell: does the book line up with God's word supported with scripture in the Bible? Are the ideas and thoughts supported by scripture; does the book teach about holiness; is Jesus mentioned as God's only begotten son? There is so much to consider when we read other books that are supposed to be related to the Word of God and we have to be prayerful when approaching these books to use as reference to the Bible.

We can use the Word of God to rightly divide the Word of truth to ourselves. The word divide here means to; dissect (expound) correctly (the divine message).

For example; one of the things I have learned is how the Secret Service identifies with counterfeit bills. The Secret Service easily identifies counterfeit money by spending a lot of time studying legal currency. So when they run across a counterfeit they can almost immediately recognize it because something in the print is out of the ordinary. In the same way, if we study the truth of the Bible, all false teachings will fail by comparison and you will recognize literature by the truth of the Bible! Knowing that the Bible was inspired (Spiritually given) by God, the Spirit of God we now have living inside of all believers will bear witness of the truth and not receive a lie.

Jesus makes a valid point to the Jews in **John 10:27** after they continued to question the validity of who

Jesus said He was several times and still they didn't understand just who He was. He said; "My sheep hear my voice, and I know them, and they follow me." Knowing the voice of God requires you to have the Spirit of God in you. The reason the Jews of that day, and even people today don't understand the scriptures is because they don't believe in Jesus as the Sod of God! Neither have they received Him as their Lord and Savior and received the gift of the Holy Spirit. This is not a suggested way of living; but a necessary requirement if you want to be counted into the fold of belonging to the Lord of Lords and the King of Kings, Jesus Christ.

Following these steps sincerely and fervently will help you to gain wisdom and understanding of God's will for your life. **Proverbs 4:5** says; "Get wisdom, Get understanding. Do not forget, nor turn away from the words of my mouth." **Proverbs 1:7** says; "The fear of the Lord is the beginning of knowledge: but fools despise wisdom and instruction." It is not enough to know of God, (wisdom); you must know Him for yourself (understanding) in a personal relationship. It is not enough to be aware of God, or a god of your understanding. You must know that God sent His Son into the world to seek and save the lost! None of us are without sin. Jesus Christ is the only one who can cleanse us, and restore us to a right relationship with God.

Just a suggestion; before you begin to study God's

word, take time to pray and ask God to open the eyes of your understanding. **Proverbs 2:1-5** says, "My son, if you receive my words, and treasure my commands within you, so that you incline your ear to wisdom, and apply your heart to understanding; Yes, if you cry out for discernment, and lift up your voice for understanding, If you seek her as silver, and search for her as for hidden treasures; Then you will understand the fear of the Lord." This fear is a reverential fear of Love, obedience and trust towards God and in His word.

It's only through God and the aid of the Holy Spirit that His word will be revealed to you, and to ask Him to reveal it is for Him to reveal Himself to you. If you desire to know God for yourself, listen for and follow after God's voice in your daily walk.

It's not an easy road, but it's worth finishing the race and keeping the faith. "We know that all things do work together for the good to those who love the Lord and those who are the called according to His purpose." **Romans 8:28**. Remember, life's journey is a walk of faith. Things won't always make sense to you, but trust in God no matter what. The study of God's word is an unending but rewarding practice.

I have a few Bibles now in my library. Wow, library! Who would have ever thought that I would utter that word one day? Anyway, I have a few books in my library now which includes a couple of Bibles with a couple of different translations. I actually started off with the Amplified Bible because it did away with those Thees and Thous, which made it complicated for me to understand. I've taken advantage of parallel Bibles with the Kings James Translation on one side of the page and the New Living Translation on the other.

With today's technology the Bible has been made available in many ways to society. I have Bible software on my computer called "BibleSoft" and it's the best! It allows me to look up partial phrases to help locate a particular scripture; it gives a variety of Bible Commentaries, dictionaries, Hebrew and Greek languages, as well as the ability to search for topics that will describe the specific meaning of a word found in the Bible that I wanted to do further research on.

Study groups are also helpful, not to get different interpretations, but different perspectives of the scriptures. Remember what **2 Peter 1:20** said about the Bible not being of any personal interpretation! In the Bible groups we should come to the same conclusion with various views because we are all distincly made as individuals, yet God's Word is universal to where we all have the same understanding, if we have the Holy Spirit living inside of us that is.

This will lead us to the final step in deliverance: walking in the Word of God.

8

Step 7: Walk

Now I must say that this chapter of the book was hardest for me to complete because I wasn't walking this out in my own life at the time. How could I write about something that I myself wasn't living out in my own life? Walking takes effort; I know from experience. This type of walking is unlike the natural stages we go through when we first come into this world. Before we walk, we crawl. Walking in the Spirit has it's similarities in that when we do become new creatures in Christ, we do become new born babes in Christ having received the Holy Spirit. The Spirit needs nutrition just as the body needs food to live. The difference is that the food that the body uses will only nourish us for a short while before we need to supply more food to sustain us, and even still, that type of nourishment for the body will eventually die out, not having the ability to sustain us but for a number of years. Spiritual nourishment however, will last throughout eternity. It is to be eaten and digested daily, especially if we want to see change in our lives. It develops us to become more like Christ and less like the person we used to be before we made a commitment to follow the ways of the Lord.

Now that I am older, I tire myself out much faster when I go for a stroll. Still, I enjoy walking because I know it's good for my health. The same thing happens when we walk with God; making the journey is difficult but the reward is everlasting. Walking in the Word of God means living, breathing, and becoming the word. Here's a definition I found on Dictionary.com on the word WALK; "To advance or travel on foot at a moderate speed or pace……" Notice the word "advance" in this definition. It implies that there is a direction that we're headed in and not just idle drifting around. Not having a plan or purpose in life will leave us walking around in a wilderness experience for years! Notice also that it mentions "moderate speed or pace" as well. While some excel quickly in their walk with the Lord; others have a slower, steadier pace. Either way progress is being made. Scripture refers to our walk as being in a race. It says that we should run with endurance or patience.

The dictionary refers to endurance as: "the fact or power of enduring or bearing pain, hardship, the ability or strength to continue or last, despite fatigue, stress or other adverse conditions." As long as we stay on the path towards the Lord, we will finish the race set before us. It's a predestinated path with signs and directions called the Holy Bible that directs us and if followed properly, we will cross that finish line some day.

II Corinthians 5:7 says; "For we walk by faith, not by sight." That journey requires believing God, and following His directions. When I get lost or confused, I turn to the book of Proverbs for guidance. For example; in the book of Proverbs it mentions that "A man's heart devises his way; but the Lord directs his steps" **Proverbs 16:9**. And "Commit thy works unto the Lord, and thy thoughts shall be established." **Proverbs 16:3**. There are many more verses in Proverbs that have aided me with my walk with the Lord and is available to you as well.

Many times, my flesh wouldn't allow me to do what God commanded. Then I turned to **Romans 7:14-20:** "For we know that the law is spiritual: but I am carnal (fleshly characteristics such as passions and appetites, sensual pleasures) and so on, sold under sin. For that which I do, I allow not: for what I would, that do I not; but what I hate, that do I. If then I do that which I would not, I consent unto the law that it is good. Now then it is no more I that do it, but sin that dwells in me. For I know that in me (that is, in my flesh,) dwells no good thing: for to will is present with me; but how to perform that which is good I find not. For the good that I would, I do not:

but the evil which I would not, that I do. Now if I do that I would not, it is no more I that do it, but sin that dwells in me."

I know that sounds like a tongue twister and believe me I must have read those verses several times before I was able to understand it. After praying and asking the Lord to make sense of it, several times, He gave me closure through the scriptures. **Galatians 5:17** helped me put things into proper perspective. It says that: "For the flesh lusteth against the Spirit, and the Spirit against the flesh: and these are contrary or (constantly fighting) the one to the other: so that ye cannot do the things that ye would."

Paul points out that the Flesh and the Spirit are always at war. He acknowledges his weaknesses and his dependence upon God through Jesus Christ. But how do we walk in the Spirit?

We do it when we practice God's word out in our lives. **Hebrews 4:12** says; "For the word of God is quick (alive), and powerful, and sharper than any two-edged sword, piercing even to the dividing asunder of soul and spirit, and of the joints and marrow, and is a discerner of the thoughts and intents of the heart."

The scripture begins with "God's word is alive." If that's true, then the word brings life to us when we apply it. **James 1:22** urges us to "Be doers of the word, and not hearers only, deceiving your own selves."

Most of us believe that if we just read a certain part of the Bible that everything will be all right and we become instant scholars. Others believe it's enough to read Psalms 23 or just display it someplace in the house or apartment while it collects dust and all will be well! But the Bible is clear; if we want to go to heaven, we must keep the commands in our hearts and live by them. **Matthew chapters 5-7,** instructs us on how we should live a Christian life. And, of course, we must come through Jesus who is the author and finisher of our faith. **Hebrews 12:2**.

He is our example of how to walk upright before God and God is Spirit and He is Truth, and they that worship Him must worship Him in Spirit and in Truth. **John 4:24**.

Hebrews 4:15 says "For we have not an high priest which cannot be touched with the feeling of our infirmities; but was in all points tempted like as we are, yet without sin." His sinless life can't be obtained by our own righteousness, because **Isaiah 64:6** says; "But we are all as an unclean thing and all our righteousness are as filthy rags; and we all do fade as a leaf; and our iniquities, like the wind, have taken us away."

Does this mean that we won't fall into sin ever again? No, but it assures us that God is near when we struggle. He will give us the victory if we don't give up seeking Him.

During my addiction, I stumbled and fell so many times that I actually lost count of how many times, but I continued to trust the Lord and his ability to set me free. After years of falling and getting back up and continuing to seek the Lord, I have obtained deliverance. You might not receive your deliverance the way or timing I received mine. But I feel God is using me to reach out to souls that are in bondage, lost and destitute of all hope, that they too may begin to follow me, "As I follow Christ."

Do I still have thoughts and desires from my past? Certainly! But that's when I hit my knees in prayer. When the craving and thoughts become overwhelming, I focus on prayer, study and just remember that I am more than a conqueror in Christ. The closer and more dependent I become on God's strength and not my own, the more peace I have in the victories that God has given me; and the less my temptations become so overwhelming to me. My fears of falling are fading day by day, not because of anything I feel that I have done, but in what I know that God has and is still doing in my life.

Although the Devil is real, I don't want to give him credit for all of my failures. **James 1:14-15** says "But every man is tempted, when he is drawn away of his own lust, and enticed, Then when lust hath conceived, it brings forth sin; and sin, when it is finished, brings forth death." I've come to also realize that everything that takes place is not always because of something we did, but it was done for the glory of God. There was a story in the gospel of John which told a story of a man that was born blind. The disciples of Jesus asked Him; "Who sinned, this man or his parents"? Jesus responded in verse 3; "Neither hath this man sinned, nor his parents: but that the works of God should be made manifest in him."

That's why the Bible encourages us to not judge someone based on appearances. God is the only righteous judge! By the way, this kind of judgment is the (condemning) judgment that pre-determines your fate based on the outward opinion and it's only God that knows the true motives of the heart. However, when we as Christians see someone who is a Christian, we do have a responsibility to correct that person for the saving of his or her soul, by the Word of God and with a meek and loving spirit. As we've already discussed, "the wages (or payment) of sin is death. **Romans 6:23**. That ultimate decision is left up to God to decide.

Now just the mention of the word "death" causes concern in people. It's a natural concern, but don't panic at the word "death." In this verse, I believe death means separation from God. However, I don't want you to be naive either, because real death can happen while we're practicing our sin out. Tomorrow is not promised to anyone!

The only reason some are still here and we know that we shouldn't be is because of the dispensation of time that God has allowed, which is grace and purpose in Him. God says that "It is not His will that any perish, but that all should come to repentance." There comes a point when you must abandon the thinking and behavior that has enslaved you and turn to Christ. He alone can liberate us from the penalty of sin, which is death both physically and spiritually. God has been long-suffering towards me. I should have been long gone from this earth, but God has spared me for His purpose.

Luke 15:12-24 tells the story of a son who wasted his inheritance living carelessly. The story doesn't get specific; it just merely states that he spent all that he had in riotess living! After he comes to himself and realizes that he could be back home with his family eating and living well, he returns to live with his father. On his return home his father is there waiting. The son acknowledged that he had sinned against heaven and against his father acknowledging that he wasn't even worthy to be called his son. Now, what happened next is a demonstration of God's love toward us. The father told his servants to bring the best robe and put it on his son, put a ring on his hand and shoes on his feet. It didn't stop there! He also cooked a good meal for his son that returned from living in sin. They threw a party for the son with dancing and music. That's how it is with God. Even though there are times in our lives when we abandon Him, God waits patiently for our return. He doesn't hold anything against us, nor does He bring any charge against us. He cast our sins into the sea of forgetfulness to be remembered no more.

He has promised that He will never leave us nor forsake us. **2 Peter 3:9**: "The Lord is not slack concerning His promise, as some men count slackness, but is long-suffering to us-ward, not willing that any should perish, but that all should come to repentance."

Remember that the focus of this book is deliverance and it's not limited to drugs or alcohol. It could be for anything that separates us from God, and sin does separate us no matter what type of sin it is. **John 8:36** says that: "if the Son therefore shall make you free, you shall be free indeed." When you don't feel free, affirm your emancipation. That's walking in faith: Believing in the impossible becoming possible through Christ. God's promises are yes and amen. Yes, he will do what he has promised if we allow Him and Amen that it is already done.

God's steadfastness actually contradicts the idea of us constantly attesting to being bound by an addiction by proclaiming, "My name is ____and I'm a ___." Your conscious decision to go back doesn't mean that God hasn't kept His promise. We have to work out our own salvation, through fear and trembling.

God delivers through prayer, time, effort and faith. Deliverance requires a personal relationship with the Lord, and trust in His promises. Deliverance takes a total commitment to God, not to our flesh and our own abilities.

Philippians 3:3 says: "For we are the circumcision, who worship God in the spirit, and rejoice in Christ Jesus, and have no confidence in the flesh." This is why it's not a good thing to say; "I need to get myself together before I come to church." Because what happens is that we're building a foundation other than the foundation that has already been built, which is Jesus Christ. Paul was a planter of churches and considered himself to be a "master builder". He identified with his position as planter; and God's as having already planted, so that Paul is more less building on something that has already existed.

In **1 Corinthians 4:10** Paul states: "According to the grace of God which is given unto me, as a wise master builder, I have laid the foundation, and another buildeth thereon. But let every man take heed how he buildeth thereupon. **V.11** For other foundation can no man lay than that is laid, which is Jesus Christ."

God promises us a new life now in this earth. But we must realize we can't do this on our own. We need a Savior, Jesus Christ.

Ephesians 2:8-10: says: "For by grace are you saved through faith; and that not of yourselves: it is the gift of God: Not of works, lest any man should boast. For we are His workmanship created in Christ Jesus unto good works, which God has before ordained that we should walk in them."

The first step in walking in newness of life is putting on Christ, being clothed in his righteousness, being cleansed by the redeeming blood of Jesus Christ that we might be reconciled back to God and be called; the righteousness of God.

Romans 10:9-10 says: "If we shall confess with our mouth the Lord Jesus, and shall believe in our heart that God has raised Him (Jesus) from the dead, that we shall be saved. For with the heart man believes unto righteousness; and with the mouth confession is made unto salvation. "

The next step is to be baptized with the baptism of repentance. That is by full submersion in water by the way, just as Jesus did in **Matthew 3:13 – 17**. That lets people know you're moving in another direction. It's an outward expression of an inward change, or a decision to change. Salvation is a continuous process. Our sinful nature went to the cross with Jesus, but we still commit acts of sin. That's why God left this provision for us in **I John 1:9**: "If we confess our sins (sincerely), He is faithful and just to forgive us our sins, and to cleanse us from all unrighteousness."

Joshua 24:15 says: "And if it seem evil unto you to serve the Lord, choose you this day whom you will serve: whether the gods which your fathers served that were on the other side of the flood, or the gods of the Amorites, in whose land you dwell: but as for me and my house, we will serve the Lord."

You can't be on both sides of the fence. **Matthew 6:24**; "No man can serve two masters: for either he will hate the one, and love the other; or else he will hold to the one, and despise the other. You cannot serve God and mammon (Money)."

All too often I hear and witness people putting too much significance on money. That in itself is a sin as stated in the Bible because it says that it's the Love of Money that is the root to all evil; **1 Timothy 6:10**. It becomes a god to some people, can't live without it, and don't realize that it chokes the very life out of them. It makes readily acceptable to take part in the pleasures of sin; instead of pleasure in God.

Revelations 3:15-16 says "I know thy works, that you are neither cold nor hot: I would that you were cold or hot, so then because you are lukewarm, (choosing to live both sides of life in the flesh and in the Spirit) and neither cold nor hot, I will spit you out of my mouth."

We all have been guilty of serving some other god, whether it be lust for sex, drugs, alcohol, money or another addiction. The question remains: which god will you serve?

If you don't know Jesus as your Lord and Savior, today is the day you can change that by confessing your sins, confessing Jesus as your Lord and Savior, and believing that He is the Son of the living God, and that Jesus now sits on the right hand of God, you shall receive the gift of the Holy Spirit that will enable you to live the life of a Christian. Would you do that today? Will you allow God to come into your heart? Will you be made whole?

Say this prayer today: Lord Jesus, I confess that I am a sinner and repent of my sins. I welcome Jesus into my heart as Lord and Savior of my life.

I believe Him to be the Son of God who raised Him from the dead and now sits at your right hand. And I believe by faith that you will send your Holy Spirit into my heart, that I may be made the righteousness of God in Christ Jesus. Amen!!! WELCOME!

CPSIA information can be obtained at www.ICGtesting.com
Printed in the USA
BVOW08s0659230114

342730BV00001B/3/P